Little People, **BIG DREAMS**
EMMELINE PANKHURST

Written by
Lisbeth Kaiser

Illustrated by
Ana Sanfelippo

Frances Lincoln
Children's Books

Emmeline was born into a big family in a nice house in Manchester, England.

At the time she grew up, life was hard for many people. Her parents did whatever they could to help, and they often brought young Emmeline along.

Emmeline learned to read when she was three, and it became her favorite thing to do. She read the newspaper and book after book, drawn to stories of heroes who fought for others. She dreamt about who she might become . . .

. . . But Emmeline didn't have many choices because she was a girl.

One night, she heard her father say that it was too bad she wasn't a boy. She wouldn't go to college, get a job, or even vote like her brothers. Emmeline didn't understand why.

She began to read about women's rights and begged her mother to bring her to a meeting so she could learn more.

There, Emmeline heard that women in England, like in many other countries, were treated unfairly. They needed the right to vote in order to change things. Emmeline knew what she had to do.

As soon as Emmeline finished high school, she began working for women's rights.

One of the leaders of the cause was a lawyer named Richard, who also believed that women should be equal to men. The two fell in love, working side by side to help women win the right to vote.

Emmeline and Richard married and had a family. For many years they tried to get voting rights for women, but nothing changed.

Sadly, Richard became sick and died, leaving Emmeline with four children, little money, and no rights as a woman.

Emmeline had to work very hard to support her family, but she didn't stop supporting women's rights.

Soon it was her daughters who begged Emmeline to take them to meetings. They asked why women had been following unfair rules for so long.

This gave Emmeline an idea . . .

Emmeline and her daughters became the leaders of a new group of women, a group that would stop following the rules and would fight for their rights. People called them suffragettes.

They started by speaking out on street corners and at fairs.
They stood up to protest at big meetings. Some people
laughed at them, but others began to listen.

The government tried to stop them, so they fought harder.
They marched in the streets. They broke windows, set fires,
and chained themselves to railings.

Even though some were hurt, and others arrested, more and more women joined Emmeline's group. They were braver than anyone had imagined.

In between spending many days in prison, Emmeline traveled
to the U.S.A. and spoke at big theaters. People gathered by
the thousands to hear her.

She told them she would keep fighting until every woman was free to do the same things as men.

Then a great war broke out, and lots of men went off to fight. Emmeline encouraged suffragettes to take over jobs that only men had done before.

They were stronger than anyone had believed.

After the war, Emmeline's dream came true: women would finally get the right to vote.

By fighting for others, Emmeline had done what no one
thought a little girl could do . . . she had become a hero.

EMMELINE PANKHURST

(Born 1858 • Died 1928)

1875 (middle)   1879

Emmeline Pankhurst was one of the world's most influential
activists who helped British women win the right to vote. Born in
Manchester, England, Emmeline was inspired at a young age by
her parents' activism and went to her first meeting about women's
rights, or "suffrage," with her mother at age 14. She soon began
working for suffrage, eventually marrying one of its leaders, Richard
Pankhurst. When Richard died unexpectedly, Emmeline raised their
four children and worked, while continuing to fight for suffrage.
Emmeline and her daughters started a new women's activist group
that encouraged women to demand their rights with "deeds not

c.1900   1928

words," protesting in ways only men had before. They were often hurt and arrested, but they kept fighting, gaining support worldwide and changing the way people thought about women. During World War One, Emmeline's suffragette army stopped protesting and took jobs that men left behind, which helped the country and showed how capable women were. The British government gave all women the right to vote shortly after Emmeline died, and many other countries followed suit. Emmeline's heroism and leadership changed the minds of an entire nation, and changed the lives of women forever.

Want to find out more about **Emmeline Pankhurst**?
Have a read of this book she wrote about her life:

Suffragette: My Own Story by Emmeline Pankhurst

If you're in England you can even visit The Pankhurst Centre, which is the
birthplace of the suffragette movement.

Quarto is the authority on a wide range of topics.
Quarto educates, entertains and enriches the lives of
our readers—enthusiasts and lovers of hands-on living.
www.quartoknows.com

First published in the U.S.A. in 2017 by Frances Lincoln Children's Books,
an imprint of The Quarto Group, 142 W 36th St, 4th Floor, New York, NY 10018, USA
QuartoKnows.com
Visit our blogs at QuartoKnows.com

Text copyright © 2017 by Lisbeth Kaiser. Illustrations copyright © 2017 by Ana Sanfelippo.

Grateful thanks to Helen Pankhurst for her consultation.

Commissioned as part of the Little People, Big Dreams series,
conceived by Mª Isabel Sánchez Vegara.
Originally published under the title Pequeña & Grande by Alba Editorial (www.albaeditorial.es)

ISBN 978-1-78603-020-7

Published by Rachel Williams • Designed by Karissa Santos
Edited by Katy Flint • Production by Kate O'Riordan
Printed in China

3 5 7 9 8 6 4

MIX
Paper from
responsible sources
FSC® C008047

Photographic acknowledgements (pages 28-29, from left to right) 1. Emmeline Pankhurst aged 17 in Geneva, 1875 © Mary Evans
Picture Library 2. A portrait of Emmeline Pankhurst, 1879 © Mary Evans Picture Library 3. Emmeline Pankhurst surrounded by police
officers, c. 1900 © Fotosearch / Stringer, Getty Images 4. Emmeline Pankhurst, 1928 © ullstein bild, Getty Images

Also in the *Little People,* **BIG DREAMS** series:

FRIDA KAHLO

ISBN: 978-1-84780-783-0

Meet Frida Kahlo, one of the best artists of the twentieth century.

COCO CHANEL

ISBN: 978-1-84780-784-7

Discover the life of Coco Chanel, the famous fashion designer.

MAYA ANGELOU

ISBN: 978-1-84780-889-9

Read about Maya Angelou—one of the world's most beloved writers.

AMELIA EARHART

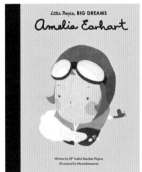

ISBN: 978-1-84780-888-2

Learn about Amelia Earhart—the first female to fly solo over the Atlantic.

AGATHA CHRISTIE

ISBN: 978-1-84780-960-5

Meet the queen of the imaginative mystery—Agatha Christie.

MARIE CURIE

ISBN: 978-1-84780-962-9

Be introduced to Marie Curie, the Nobel Prize-winning scientist.

ROSA PARKS

ISBN: 978-1-78603-018-4

Discover the life of Rosa Parks, the first lady of the civil rights movement.

AUDREY HEPBURN

ISBN: 978-1-78603-053-5

Learn about the iconic actress and humanitarian—Audrey Hepburn.

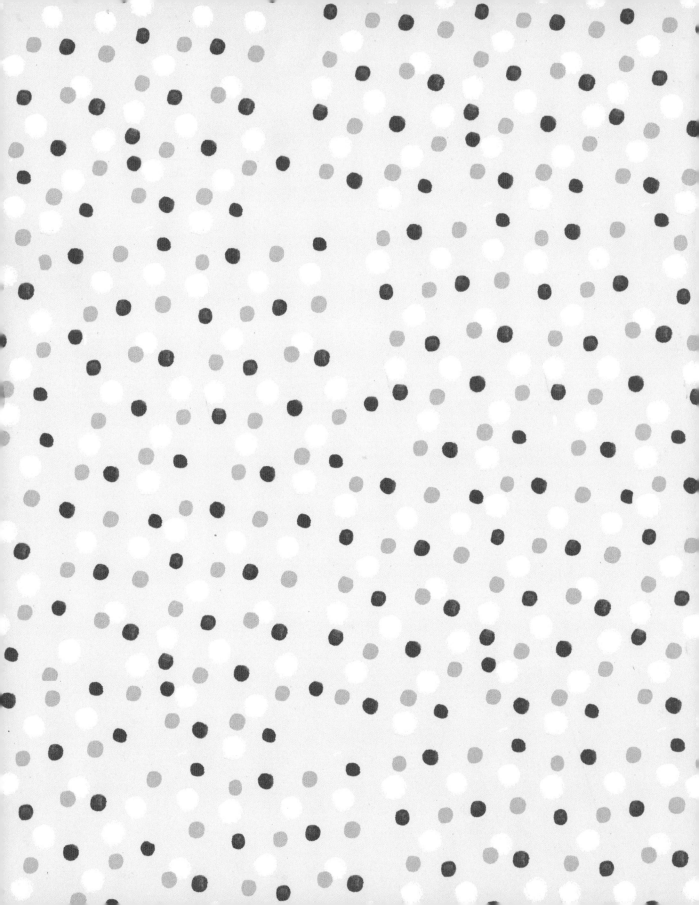